My First Animal Library

# Opossums

by Mari Schuh

Bullfrog
Books

# Ideas for Parents and Teachers

Bullfrog Books let children practice reading informational text at the earliest reading levels. Repetition, familiar words, and photo labels support early readers.

## Before Reading

- Discuss the cover photo. What does it tell them?

- Look at the picture glossary together. Read and discuss the words.

## Read the Book

- "Walk" through the book and look at the photos. Let the child ask questions. Point out the photo labels.

- Read the book to the child, or have him or her read independently.

## After Reading

- Prompt the child to think more. Ask: Have you ever seen an opossum? Where were you? What was the animal doing?

Bullfrog Books are published by Jump!
5357 Penn Avenue South
Minneapolis, MN 55419
www.jumplibrary.com

Library of Congress Cataloging-in-Publication Data

Schuh, Mari C., 1975– author.
 Opossums / by Mari Schuh.
    pages cm. — (My first animal library)
 Audience: Ages 5–8.
 Audience: K to grade 3.
 Summary: "Vibrant photographs and carefully leveled text introduce emergent readers to an opossum as hunts for food, defends itself against predators, and raises its young. Includes labeled diagram, picture glossary, and index."—Provided by publisher.
  ISBN 978-1-62031-289-6 (hardcover: alk. paper) —
  ISBN 978-1-62496-349-0 (ebook)
 1. Opossums—Juvenile literature.  I. Title.
 II. Series: Bullfrog books. My first animal library.
 QL737.M34S38 2016
 599.2'76—dc23
                                                2015028801

Editor: Jenny Fretland VanVoorst
Series Designer: Ellen Huber
Book Designer: Michelle Sonnek
Photo Researcher: Michelle Sonnek

Photo Credits: All photos by Shutterstock except: age fotostock, 18–19; Alamy, cover, 20–21; Corbis, 22; Dreamstime, 1, 6–7; Getty, 16–17; Tony Alter, 13.

Printed in China.

For Rye and John—MS

# Table of Contents

# Night Hunters

Night is here.

An opossum wakes up.
She leaves her den.

She climbs a tree.

She hunts for food.

Her long tail helps her climb.
She grabs tree branches.

**Look! She finds eggs. Yum!**

Opossums are not picky.

They eat dead animals.

They eat garbage, too.

# Oh no! A fox!

Hiss! Hiss!

The opossum shows her teeth.

Then she plays dead.

Bye, fox!

The opossum is safe.

She waddles home.

The opossum gives birth
in her den.

The babies are tiny.

Each one is the size
of a bee.

The babies crawl
to mom's pouch.

They drink milk.

They grow.

pouch

baby

They climb onto mom's back.

Time for a ride!

Whee!

# Parts of an Opossum

**body**
Opossums are about the size of a house cat.

**fur**
Opossums are covered with long fur.

**snout**
Opossums have a long snout, much like a rat.

**tail**
An opossum's long tail wraps around tree branches.

# Picture Glossary

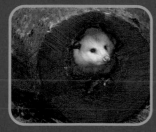

**den**
A wild animal's home; opossum dens are often in hollow trees.

**pouch**
A flap of skin that looks like a bag or pocket where some animals carry their young.

**hunt**
To look for animals to eat.

**waddle**
To take short steps and move from side to side.

# Index

# To Learn More

Learning more is as easy as 1, 2, 3.

1) Go to www.factsurfer.com

2) Enter "opossums" into the search box.

3) Click the "Surf" button to see a list of websites.

With factsurfer.com, finding more information is just a click away.